CODE BREAKERS AND SPIES

Code Breakers and Spies of
the American
Revolution

CASSANDRA SCHUMACHER

Cavendish
Square
New York

Library of Congress Cataloging-in-Publication Data

Names: Schumacher, Cassandra, author.
Title: Code breakers and spies of the American Revolution / Cassandra Schumacher.
Description: First edition. | New York : Cavendish Square, 2018. | Series: Code breakers and spies | Includes bibliographical references and index. | Audience: Grade 7 to 12.
Identifiers: LCCN 2017048052 (print) | LCCN 2017058227 (ebook) | ISBN 9781502638465 (ebook) | ISBN 9781502638441 (library bound) | ISBN 9781502638458 (pbk.)
Subjects: LCSH: United States--History--Revolution, 1775-1783--Secret service--Juvenile literature. | Espionage--United States--History--18th century--Juvenile literature. | Spies--United States--History--18th century--Juvenile literature.
Classification: LCC E279 (ebook) | LCC E279 .S38 2018 (print) | DDC 973.3/85--dc23
LC record available at https://lccn.loc.gov/2017048052

Editorial Director: David McNamara
Editor: Stacy Orlando
Copy Editor: Alex Tessman
Associate Art Director: Amy Greenan
Designer: Alan Sliwinski
Production Coordinator: Karol Szymczuk
Photo Research: J8 Media

The photographs in this book are used by permission and through the courtesy of: Cover, p. 1 FernandoAH/ E+/Getty Images; p. 4 Interim Archives/Getty Images; p. 8 George Washington/Wikimedia Commons/ File:Washington Pennsylvania Map.jpg; p. 11 Sipley/ClassicStock/Getty Images; p. 20 Gift of Walter P. Chrysler, Jr., in honor of Walter P. Chrysler, Sr./Wikimedia Commons/ File:Washington Crossing the Delaware 185671 George Caleb Bingham.jpg; p. 24 New York Review of Books, June 23, 2011/Wikimedia Commons/ File:EdwardBancroft.jpg; p. 28 Bettmann/Getty Images; p. 32 Ralph Earl/Wikimedia Commons/ File:Benjamin Tallmadge by Ralph Earl.jpeg; p. 36 Universal History Archive/UIG via Getty Images; p. 41 https://www. flickr.com/photos/pmlib/4745932357/Wikimedia Commons/ File:Austin Roe.jpg; p. 45 Benjamin Tallmadge/ Wikimedia Commons/ File:Culper Ring code.jpg; p. 47 Thomas Hart/Wikimedia Commons/ File:Benedict Arnold 1color.jpg; p. 49 Stock Montage/ Archive Photos/Getty Images; p. 50 Lafayette College Art Collection/ Wikimedia Commons/ File:Armistead and Lafayette by Jean Baptiste Le; p. Paon 1783.jpg; p. 52 PHAS/UIG via Getty Images; p. 57 White House Historical Association/Wikimedia Commons/ File:Thomas Jefferson by Rembrandt Peale, 1800.jpg; p. 63 Giorgio Rossi/Shutterstock.com; p. 65 ezphoto/Shutterstock.com.

Printed in the United States of America

Contents

Map No. 4.

NORTH AMERICA

1750.

SHOWING CLAIMS ARISING OUT OF EX-
PLORATION AND OCCUPANCY.

English   French

Spanish

LONGMANS, GREEN & CO.

STIRRINGS OF WAR

The stories of the formation of the Continental Congresses, the Declaration of Independence, and George Washington's role in the birth of America are topics widely taught. What few people discuss are the men and women who helped fight the war behind the scenes. It was not simply the army that won the war for freedom; it was the spies that tipped the balance. Spying in the 1700s was not like it is today and had many challenges. The landscape of the country was young and wild, and without the benefits of electronics, computers, phones, or transportation beyond horseback and a

OPPOSITE:
This map shows the European colonial divisions of North America in 1750.

person's own two feet, information was difficult to gather and traveled very slowly.

Spying behind enemy lines was ultimately Washington's best weapon in the American Revolution. He learned this weapon long before the first shots at Lexington and Concord rang out. Perhaps the best way to examine the obstacles early spies had to overcome is to look at their accomplishments. Espionage in the United States started in the French and Indian War when a younger, less experienced Washington was sent on a mission into Ohio territory.

The Making of a Spy Master

In 1753, George Washington inherited his late brother's officer's commission in the British military. In the 18th century, it was common for families to buy officer positions in the military so their sons would have respectable jobs. When Washington's brother died, there was an open commission as an officer owned by his family that Washington was able to take over. The French were pushing into territory the British already viewed as theirs in the Ohio Valley, and newly appointed Washington was moved into battle. Lieutenant Governor Robert Dinwiddie was charged by King George II to keep the French at bay.

Rather than build the recommended forts, Dinwiddie elected for some small-scale espionage first.

He enlisted the help of young Washington to deliver a letter to the French warning them off further movement and encouraging them to leave the region. This delivery would serve a dual purpose, because Dinwiddie also asked Washington to take note of the French military resources. Washington was told to collect information on weaponry and arms, troop numbers, fort defenses, and different communications and plans.

Handwritten Notes on the Venango Path

Washington's observations began in Venango, a Native American town, where he met with French officers for dinner. Washington gathered as much intelligence as he could. A bit of alcohol loosened the tongues of the officers, and Washington received some valuable military information. He drew maps of the areas he traveled, and noted that there were somewhere between six to seven hundred soldiers amongst four forts. The fort constructed at Venango was designed to keep the English settlers away from that area. The second, Fort Le Boeuf, was where Washington was headed. A third, Fort Niagara, located on Lake Erie, was being

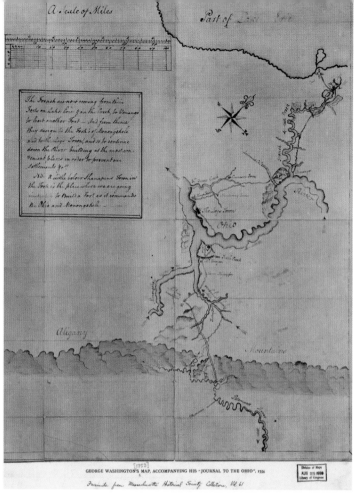

George Washington used this map while spying in Ohio during the French and Indian War.

used to store supplies from further up in Canada, specifically Montreal. Additionally, there were three outposts between Montreal to help guard the trade route. The last fort was on Lake Ontario. While not seemingly a lot, the French military resources showed that they were looking to stay.

Washington continued on to Fort Le Boeuf where he met Captain Jacques Legardeur de Saint-Pierre and

Captain Repentigny and presented the letter. There, he examined the fort's defenses. He made illustrations, recording the shape of the fort's walls, and drew the location as an area almost entirely surrounded by water. He noted the defenses like weaponry and placement of portholes for firing cannons through, and all the designs of the fort that help with defense. There were about one hundred soldiers in addition to the officers. Most interesting to Washington were the canoes, both completed and under construction at the fort. The French had collected 220 canoes with more in the works. The preparations at the fort implied that the French were planning to travel the Ohio River and expand their presence, moving further into what King George II deemed English territory.

The Power of Misdirection

Using Washington's information, Dinwiddie rushed to have a fort constructed at the fork of the Monongahela River to keep the French at bay. Washington, who had been awarded a promotion to Lieutenant for his information during his stay at Fort Le Boeuf, was charged with stocking the fort with ready militia and found his first experience in battle. Washington also ordered the construction of Fort Necessity.

It was at Necessity that Washington began his next foray into espionage, specifically the spreading of false information. He circulated a propaganda letter among French soldiers that listed the benefits of deserting the French side to the British. Deserters would not only weaken the French, but also had valuable military intelligence that Washington could use.

The French, having learned Washington was looking for allies, sent a party of Native Americans in an attempt to spy on the fort. Washington told them fake information, which the Native Americans brought back to the French. Washington lied about his own plans and resources and misled the French. He was becoming better at espionage, but still had trouble gaining intel on the French's resources and plans. Lack of information, and Fort Necessity's imperfect location surrounded by forest and hills, would lead to one of Washington's most humiliating military defeats.

On July 3, 1754, Captain Louis Coulon de Villiers attacked the fort. Washington's troops were not prepared, and recent rains had impeded weaponry. There was little defense against the French forces. Hostages were taken, and Washington was forced to surrender—the only time he ever did. Coulon blamed Washington for the death of his brother in a previous battle, and unbeknownst to Washington, the

This depiction shows a young George Washington at Fort Duquesne during the French and Indian War.

surrender document also contained a clause declaring him responsible. Washington unwittingly signed, and was humiliated when the French published the document along with his journal later on. Though not formally chastised and thanked by the Virginia House of Burgesses and Governor Dinwiddie, when the Virginia Regiment was disbanded, Washington was placed in a reduced role and ranked as Captain in his new Virginia force. The hit to his rank led Washington to resign his commission.

Valuable Lessons

Washington returned to battle in 1755 when he negotiated an aid-de-camp position to work alongside English Major General Edward Braddock. Washington was able to keep his pride, not lose his rank, and also work within the mandate that colonial officers had to be two ranks lower than the commanding British officer. Unfortunately for Washington, Braddock was not strategically minded, had little actual military experience, and did not have the couth to work well with Native American allies. Furthermore, Braddock simply did not understand the limitations of the American frontier and was very poorly equipped to travel the terrain. He traveled with the traditional European military entourage of camp followers, baggage, and cumbersome, heavy, artillery.

DID YOU KNOW?

Washington was strongly focused on accuracy in information and required that informants double and triple check the truth of their information before sending it on to him.

His troops were poorly trained. Overall, the group was not prepared for battle and the challenge of marching over marshy lands and mountainous topography. While traveling to Fort Cumberland, Braddock was forced to change his methodology, choosing to separate his two thousand men into two parties. The first sector would be able to travel much faster because the second group would carry the artillery.

Though one problem had been solved, about 10 miles (16 kilometers) outside of Fort Duquesne, the French attacked. The red coats of the British and adherence to European tactics were not successful in the forest environment. The soldiers were easy to pick off. The poor military planning meant the men were not prepared for battle like the French and Native Americans were. The more naturally colored attire of the Native Americans concealed them in the trees, and the French were more organized. At the end of the battle, Braddock was mortally wounded and the British had lost close to 70 percent of their men. Washington, however, had learned a valuable lesson as a military man: proper planning and troop preparation were important, but scouting, reconnaissance, deception, propaganda, and good military intelligence were the keys to success. It was during the French and Indian War that America's first spy master was born.

On the Eve of War

People in the American colonies lived in different states under British rule since the founding of the first colony in 1607. One hundred years of occupation had created certain expectations between Americans and the British. Colonists had their own local governments. They lived on farms, plowing fields with thick metal plows, growing food, and raising livestock. Large cities were continuing to grow, developing infrastructure and relatively independent economies. Colonists would pick up a quill, ink, and paper in order to write letters that traveled the seas for weeks in order for information to reach the motherland. A cup or two of good British tea were sipped in a drawing room or kitchen, and life went on.

Colonists picked up their guns and fought alongside the British in the French and Indian War, but it was an unspoken understanding that the colonies were relatively independent. Occasionally a tax would arise to help regulate trade and protect British interests. The cost of the French and Indian War changed that. The British started passing more taxes on Americans, and justified it because debt had been accrued protecting the American properties.

Unrest Grows

King George III imposed a series of taxes on the colonies that met serious resistance and inadvertently led to the revolution. For instance, the Stamp Act of 1765, which taxed paper products and stamps, was not about trade regulation, but was simply a way to make money on the colonists' letters. The tax was not high, but Americans were not comfortable with being a source of income for the crown without any consent or vote on their part. Parliament was forced to repeal the act after mob violence broke out. Colonists wanted a representative in Parliament, and otherwise felt the taxes to be unlawful.

The Declaratory Act (1766) that followed the reaction to the Stamp Act told colonists that the British Parliament could tax the colonies at will. It said Great Britain ruled and could make laws over the colonies in any way, shape, or form regardless of the American colonists' consent. Parliament then passed the Townshend Acts (1767), which suspended the New York colony's government until the colonists met the terms of the Quartering Act (1765), where colonists had to house British soldiers in barracks in any available, empty shelter created and funded by the colonists. It also taxed household luxuries like paint, lead, glass, paper, and most famous of all, tea.

Colonists protested again, and Parliament repealed all the duties but the one on tea in 1770. Things were tense, but relatively peaceful until 1773 and the passing of the Tea Act. This act gave exclusive tea trade rights in the colonies to the East India Trading Company which, paired with the remaining tax from the Townsend Act, made American blood boil and, in Boston, boil over.

The Underground in Action

On the eve of December 16, 1773, Samuel Adams and the Sons of Liberty, an underground colonial organization, disguised themselves as Native Americans and boarded three East India Company ships parked in the Boston Harbor. Colonists tossed 342 chests of very expensive English tea in protest (to the tune of what would equal $1 million in modern US dollars) during what became known as the Boston Tea Party. The hand of the crown came down heavy with the Coercive Acts of 1774.

Designed to punish the unruly Bostonians, the Boston port was to be closed until damages were paid back to the East India Trading Company. The crown took back control of the government of

The Spy in the Sons of Liberty

With tensions rising in Massachusetts after the Boston Tea Party, the Commander of the British Forces in North America, Thomas Gage, needed a spy who moved quietly and comfortably through the colony. Dr. Benjamin Church was just the ticket. Church appeared to be an upstanding patriot as a member of the Sons of Liberty and would eventually be the chief surgeon of the Continental army. The English pounds offered by Gage, however, loosened his tongue and he told his secrets and sold them to the British.

Unfortunately for Church, his spy career ended rather quickly when a coded letter fell into patriot hands early on. The letter was ultimately presented to George Washington who turned it over to two forerunning code breakers of the revolution, Reverend Samuel West and Colonel Elisha Porter. Their efforts cracked the code and condemned Church. Though the physician swore until his death that he had provided false information to the British as a sort of double agent, his profiteering off the British made him look like a spy. Church was found to be guilty, but the Continental Congress had not made spying illegal yet (this would be remedied quickly thereafter). Church was imprisoned until he was exiled to the West Indies in 1780. His ship was lost at sea.

Massachusetts with a loyal British governor at the head. Moreover, British officials could no longer be criminally prosecuted in Massachusetts, and the Quartering Act was extended so that British soldiers were to be welcomed in colonists' homes on demand. As a further insult to steadfast American Protestants, the Coercive Acts gave Canadians the freedom to practice Catholicism. The crown's goal was to alienate Bostonians and New England from the colonies and quiet the discontent. Instead, it lit the match that would fuel the revolution.

Spying in the Era of the Revolution

As evidenced by Washington's first forays into spying, espionage of the eighteenth century was not what it is today. Not only were the methods simpler without modern computers, telephones, and general amenities that we use every single day and in their place quills and letters, but the very act of spying took more time. Short trips like Washington's journey to Fort Le Boeuf were standard spy activity, and the traveling alone could take weeks. Spies would use technology like hand-drawn maps, coded letters, and invisible inks to both share information and hinder opponents and enemies from discovering their secrets, but intelligence gathering was not much of a long-term game. It often involved quick forays into enemy territory with some level of military transparency. For example, Washington did not conceal his alliance with the English while wandering into French territory, and was open about his goal to deliver a letter written by the English to the French. He gathered valuable intelligence that was in turn delivered to his supervisors while there, but it was not a planned subterfuge. This does not mean that spies were not at times hidden within plain sight of the enemy, but that espionage was more gentlemanly in nature. Spies operated under the concepts of honor like gentleman and soldiers of the time. In some ways, the American Revolution would change the methods and face of espionage.

THE REVOLUTION

B efore the American Revolution began in 1775, the colonies were at an international disadvantage. Britain had provided many of their imported resources, and new sources of support during the war effort were necessary. To provide international trade and dealings, the Committee of Correspondence was established in 1772, which would become the Committee of Secret Correspondence. Names like Benjamin Harrison, Thomas Paine, and John Jay are associated with the committee, but the most productive and active member was Benjamin Franklin. In a series of secret letters, Franklin

OPPOSITE:
George Washington and his troops crossed the Delaware River to Trenton to defeat the Hessians.

reached out to his extensive list of international contacts including members of the Spanish royal family and American sympathizers in France. He made contact with France's Julien-Alexander Archard de Bonvouloir, who was sent by France to secretly seek out and speak with the Continental Congress. Their meeting encouraged France's support during the war. It created an agreement where Americans would provide resources and commodities to France in exchange for arms and military supplies.

International Intrigue and Foreign Affairs

The thirteen colonies sent Silas Dean of Connecticut as a liaison to France, but he was poorly suited to the international component of the work. He did not speak French and did not travel abroad. Dr. Edward Bancroft was enlisted as an assistant to Dean. Unfortunately, Bancroft's loyalties were to the British and he was contacted by British Spy Master Paul Wentworth. As a gambler with a history of bad investments, he needed the financial compensation the crown could provide in exchange for information. Bancroft gave just enough information to America to ensure his own cover, but provided the British with a near-to-direct line of information on the agreements between France and America. He was very dangerous to America's relationships in France.

Propaganda Abroad

Needing further support, Franklin released fake pamphlets in France that detailed how the British were allegedly paying Native Americans for patriot scalps. Then, when the British started making moves toward peace in 1778, Franklin provided more false information about possible reconciliation between the Americans and British that would result in both parties taking up arms against France. Though there was no chance of reconciliation and the goal was always independence, the possibility was enough to get France to ally with America so that reunification would not take place. That alliance between colonists and France was a huge turning point in the war.

During this time, Bancroft kept the British well informed to the point where the king of England had a copy of the treaty between Americans and the French two days after it was written. Using ciphers, secret ink, and cover letters where the information was written in between the lines of a fake letter in invisible ink, Bancroft provided extensive information to the British. The letters were dead dropped, a process

Dr. Edward Bancroft was a double agent for the British in France during the revolution.

where one spy would hide information in a predetermined location for pick up by another spy. Bancroft shoved his letters into a bottle hung in a hole in a tree where another intelligence agent would later pick it up. Interestingly, the Crown never really acted on the information provided by Bancroft out of fear of war with France. They could not afford to stretch their resources any further and starting a war with France would have been the only real way to stop the secret arms trade with the colonies.

Bancroft was only suspected once as a spy and that was by Arthur Lee, another member of the Committee of Secret Correspondence. Lee was known to be grumpy and unpleasant and was therefore not taken seriously when he presented his evidence to the other members of the committee. There is some evidence, however, that Benjamin Franklin did believe Lee's accusation and also knew Bancroft was a spy, but rather than expose him, Franklin chose to use him. Bancroft was a great tool to fuel British anger that might have led to war with France. He could report back information that led to decreasing military presence in the Americas, or knowledge of France's alliance with America, which would encourage the British to pull out of America sooner. If it was true that Franklin knew about Bancroft, then he was not only a great patriot, but possibly one of the most cunning international manipulators of all time.

By Land or By Sea

As tensions with Britain were mounting, the American Sons of Liberty in Boston tightened the screw. One specific patriot and Son of Liberty took notice and action. Most famous for his midnight ride to alert the Americans of the coming British forces before the battles of Lexington and Concord, Paul Revere is an esteemed patriot. What he is less known for is his extensive spying operation. Starting shortly after the passage of the Stamp Act in 1766 and hitting its most extensive numbers between 1774 and 1775, famed Revere was operating the first layman's spy ring of the American Revolution.

Citizen Reconnaissance

Known as the Mechanics or the Liberty Boys, this team consisted of artisans and skilled laborers dedicated to the cause. Revere had amassed a group of thirty different individuals who spent their evenings watching British troops and their activities. They worked in teams of two and watched the patrols for changes in behavior. They would even steal and sabotage British equipment. While not particularly good at spying (they were infiltrated by British spy Benjamin Church), they did discover the British plan to move seven hundred troops to Concord so that they could take American military supplies. Such a move would have essentially shut down the uprising before it could truly begin.

Seeing the movement toward Concord, Revere was charged with alerting patriots in Lexington of the British army's activity. They needed to be warned that Lexington would also be a likely target. In a famed moment of American history, Revere chose to use lanterns to signal British movement whether it was by land or by sea. If one lantern was hung, the British were making a land attack; if two lanterns were hung, the British were moving by water. Watchmen hung two lanterns in the steeple of the local church, which told Revere that the British were traveling by sea.

Revere, along with two other patriots, Dr. Samuel Prescott and Williams Dawes, made the famed ride toward Lexington and Concord to spread the news. They notified people in the network of the coming

British through prearranged signals like church bells, drums, and gun signals that declared the British were on the move. It helped word travel quickly. Unfortunately during the ride, the men were apprehended by the British, and Revere was detained. The other two, however, managed to sneak away and continued on to alert the men at Concord of the British plan, essentially saving the revolution. The patriots at Concord were able to move the supplies they had stored, saving their supplies, and the troops there were prepared for the first skirmish that officially began the war.

Spying on the Home Front

Washington had learned the value of good information during the French and Indian War, and he knew he would need a formal spy system during the revolution. The British military was more experienced, well-funded, and allied with the German Hessians who were very well trained. It was going to be a challenge to defeat them by sheer might. Washington needed to fight a strategic battle based on valuable and accurate information. He needed spies.

In 1775, the first moves toward military intelligence were taken when Washington enlisted William Duer, a member of the Continental Congress, to discretely

The British hanged American Nathan Hale as a spy on September 22, 1776.

seek out men to gather intelligence for the patriots, specifically in British-occupied New York. Men sent directly in for information were quickly ferreted out and unsuccessful. They were detected by the British as spies and did not gather much information. The primary objective at this time was to gather intelligence and not necessarily set up an espionage system. Spying was an evening activity where the spy would return to camp by dawn the next day, but that system was not working for Washington.

Espionage was off to a slow start in America. Though Washington had high hopes and desired a strong intelligence network, things were not going to plan. It was during this period that one of America's most famous and least effective spies, Nathan Hale, was in Washington's service.

In Disguise

Nathan Hale was sent into New York under the disguise of being an unemployed schoolteacher to try to discover the British plans in Long Island and discover how the region felt about the revolution. The Hessian colonel, Robert Rogers, suspected that young Hale was not in New York on such innocent business and began investigating. Rogers set out to befriend and dupe Hale to discover his true plans.

Over what seemed to be good company, a bit of drink, and dinner, Hale told his new friends of his real purposes for being in New York. Rogers listened carefully to Hale's mission of spying in Long Island while his troops surrounded the house, entrapping the young Hale. Hale was placed under arrest. On September 22, 1776, without a trial, Nathan Hale was executed as a spy against the British in New York. It marked a dark period in spying for the Americans. It was hard to get a reliable man anywhere near New York.

Behind Enemy Lines

Setting up a sound network of spies was necessary but challenging due to the ever-changing locations of the army. Even worse, the British military was gradually gaining more land. General John Burgoyne had sent a hidden letter to General William Howe in a hollowed out quill that described his plans for Philadelphia. Though this letter made it to its intended recipient, the reply was not so lucky. The return letter intercepted from General William Howe told Washington that the British were heading to Philadelphia and Washington needed good information even sooner.

The need for intelligence was only growing, not lessening, so Washington charged Colonel John Cadwalader to send out spies to seek out intelligence and asked William Alexander, Lord Sterling, to find someone willing to cross the river from New Jersey to New York. Cadwalader's source noted that the British were south of Trenton just across the Delaware River in New York. The Hessians that were near were also prepared, and both parties were far too close to Washington's position in New Jersey. The insecure location and encroaching winter weather had Washington nervous and he knew he had to work quickly.

Guided by the intel from his spy, Washington decided to divide his troops three ways and cross the Delaware to wage a surprise attack on the Hessians at Trenton. In one of the most famous moves of the American Revolution, the crossing of the Delaware on the night of December 25, 1776, gave Washington and his troops a win over the far better trained Hessian mercenaries. Washington, a careful and suspicious man, kept the plan almost entirely to himself to ensure that no British spy could alert the enemy. The victory over the Hessians was the first victory of the war and was an important turning point because of the way it raised morale. It showed that the Continental Army, while physically weaker, stood a chance to win even if the odds were against them.

Starting Spy Rings

Nathan Hale's execution marked a changing tone in spying during the revolution as well. British spies were treated with little remorse and quickly sentenced to the noose. In a way, Hale's death had turned into a martyrdom that would inspire greater caution and success in the coming years as far as spies were concerned. Coming off the success at Trenton,

DID YOU KNOW?

British General Henry Clinton was one of the more forgiving of generals during the war and did not execute spies.

Benjamin Tallmadge was the first member of the Culper Ring.

Washington was pushing for effective, accurate intelligence with the turning year.

At Washington's urging, Continental Congressman Willian Duer recommended Nathaniel Sackett, a colleague from the same committee, to create a network of spies. For $500 and a stipend of $50 a month, Washington hired his first spy chief.

The first addition to Sackett's team was Benjamin Tallmadge, a friend of the late Nathan Hale. Tallmadge, relatively new to the military, enlisted in 1776, but moved up quickly in rank and was based out of Connecticut by 1777. He was enrolled as a dragoon during the day and would spend his evenings running espionage across Long Island Sound. He completed jobs like ferrying Major John Clark, who was known for being good with gathering information on enemy military, into Long Island, which was still held by the British. Clark reported back to Tallmadge during his months in Setauket, Long Island, about the British military placement while blending in with and learning the ways of the British army. Setauket would become pivotal in one of the most successful spy rings of the revolution.

Undercover Operatives

Nathaniel Sackett, however, was not as accomplished at gathering information as he was at creating ways to spy. Sackett is credited as the first in American espionage to utilize disguise for long-term spying. Sackett sent a man into New York under the disguise of being a poultry salesman, and so was born the concept of infiltrating the enemy long term. He also recruited a Hessian deserter to talk other Hessians into doing the same.

Sackett was also the first spy leader to use a woman for intelligence, though not by intentionally employing her. Apparently, the woman's husband had allied with the British, and their grain had been stolen. The woman initially complained to Sackett who sent her to speak with General Howe. Of course, Howe was unable to help and the woman returned to Sackett with the complaint that odds were nothing would be done. Instead of helping loyalists in the city, she noted that the many flat-bottomed boats in the harbor of New York were going to be used to ferry British soldiers to Philadelphia where they would take the city from the Americans. Her unintentional assistance helped America avoid that conflict!

Encoded Messages

Ciphers were a great military tool used by both sides of the fight during the revolution. A key would be created where one or more symbols would stand in for the letters of the alphabet and different numbers. The more symbols that stood for a letter, the harder the code was to break.

The cipher creator would send a key to the recipient of the secret letter in advance and then use it to transcribe the letter. What is interesting is that basic cipher technology used all the way back during the revolution would eventually lead to modern computers. The binary code that computers use to store data consists of sequences of zeroes and ones. It is essentially a very modern, commonly used cipher.

Ultimately, Sackett left his secretive service shortly thereafter, but not without leaving his stamp on espionage. He had also laid the groundwork for the formation of one of America's most famous spy rings: the Culper Ring.

The Culper Ring

When Nathaniel Sackett recruited Benjamin Tallmadge, he gave Washington a gift that would pay out in the coming years. Tallmadge was the head of the Culper spy ring. Named for Culpeper County where Washington grew up, the Culper Ring ran out of Setauket, Long Island. Formed in the summer of 1778, the small ring consisted of six men and one woman, and was very well concealed. Members and intelligence were designated by numbers and code names rather than their birth names to preserve the safety of the members.

The Culper Ring would use some of the most advanced technologies as well as some of the simplest tools to spread information to one another so it could make it back to Washington as quickly as possible. The only way intelligence was valuable was if it could make it to Washington quickly enough for him to act on it. From invisible ink known as sympathetic stain to complex ciphers, the ring used the latest technologies available to them.

DID YOU KNOW?

Washington did not know all of the members of the Culper Ring or their names. Members worked hard to remain anonymous even to the people with whom they worked.

SPYING IN THE REVOLUTION

Intercepted messages were a valuable tool during the war that both sides used. Black chambers were set up to help the generals read the mail of opposing sides. The term "black chamber" simply referred to any room in a post office where military letters would be read for information and copied without the knowledge of the writer or recipient. Mail from the enemy's side would be opened so that the letters could be transcribed and ciphered. Then, the original letter would be carefully resealed so that it seemed like it had never been opened and sent on

OPPOSITE:
British General Burgoyne surrendered to American forces at Saratoga.

to its intended recipient. The copied letter would be read for valuable information.

Ciphers, Codes, and Secrets

To keep their enemies from reading their letters, spies would encrypt and code their letters. Ciphers would be used to hide the contents of letters, but spies also used masks and grilles. A letter would be written that appeared to talk about a different topic, but the truth was revealed with a mask or a grille. A mask was another sheet of paper with a pattern cut out of it to reveal the important parts of the letters. The mask would be placed over the letter and only the true message would be visible. The mask would be sent separately from the letter in case the letter fell into the wrong hands. Without the proper mask, the message of the letter was lost on the unwanted reader. Some letters were even designed to fall into enemy hands to provide false information that would trick the other side.

Hidden Messages

Both Britain and America had ways of hiding information from one another. For example, when the British spy Captain Daniel Taylor was apprehended by patriots, he had a small, silver ball screwed together to hide a message written on a piece of silk. When the patriots caught him, Taylor swallowed the ball. The American General Horatio Gates had his soldiers give Taylor a medicine that would make him vomit. The ball came out, but Taylor quickly swallowed it again. Gates threatened to cut the ball out of Taylor's stomach. Instead, Taylor took the medicine again and Gates got the message.

The metal ball Taylor swallowed was an example of a hidden letter. Letters would also be hidden in seemingly unrelated objects. Hollowed-out quills or buttons could hide messages, and never be noticed.

Most interesting of all the different tools is probably the sympathetic stain and other invisible inks. Spies would send messages to one another by writing in books, on pamphlets, or even between the lines of unrelated letters in invisible ink. Many of the invisible inks used before the revolution were based on foods like lemon juice which, when heated, reveals the message to the reader. During the war, English physician James Jay created what Washington called sympathetic stain. Sympathetic stain required a chemical reaction between the agent used to write the letter and the reagent to make the words visible. The letter could only be read once the reagent was brushed over the hidden words making them visible. Jay used gallnut ink for the stain and ferrous sulfate for the reagent.

The Clark Spy Ring

Operating slightly before the Culper Ring was in New York, the Clark Spy Ring was working in Philadelphia. Major John Clark Jr. organized a ring of spies that bedeviled General William Howe and his efforts to gain Philadelphia. The ring released false information to Howe's army and kept Washington informed of British movement in the area. It was because of Clark that Washington was aware of loyalist sentinels along every route, land and water, into Philadelphia.

The Clark Ring also informed Washington of British movement leaving the city of Philadelphia to attack the Continental Army. This foreknowledge allowed Washington to prepare his army. When the British arrived at White Marsh, the Americans were prepared and the British could not draw them into a major battle as they had planned. After a few short skirmishes, General Howe gave up and withdrew to Philadelphia out of frustration.

Clark even provided intel on British movement while Washington was camped at Valley Forge.

Though Washington did not have facilities to act on any British raiding because of the terrible conditions at Valley Forge, he was informed of what was going on. It was only with Clark's failing health that he left military service and that spy ring came to an end.

Members of the Culper Ring

Austin Roe transported letters as a courier for the Culper Spy Ring.

The Culper Ring solved one of Washington's biggest problems by finding someone in loyalist New York to send out military information. The ring consisted of very few members, each with their own code name or number. Benjamin Tallmadge was known by the alias John Bolton or the number 721. Robert Townsend was Samuel Culper Jr. or code number 723. Abraham Woodhull was Samuel Culper Sr. and number 722. Austin Roe was known as number 724. Caleb Brewster was represented with 725, and the ring leader himself, Agent 711, George Washington. Anna Strong was the only female in the ring and known by the number 355. The most unlikely member was James Rivington, a loyalist turned patriot.

Abraham Woodhull was recruited by Tallmadge and was a nervous man inspired by the loss of a distant cousin to join the war effort. He became a spy to avenge his cousin against the British. He was also the primary source of intelligence out of Setauket to Washington.

Samuel Culper Sr. answered Washington's questions about the strength and numbers of the British in New York. He would go into the city on alleged business and to visit his sister and her husband. His real reason to visit New York was to gather military intelligence and send the information back to Washington.

Austin Roe was a farmer who owned a tavern in Setauket. His cow field was beside Woodhull's, and their cows shared a pasture. He carried letters to and

DID YOU KNOW?

It was Benjamin Tallmadge who uncovered that Benedict Arnold was a traitor trying to sell out West Point to Major John André of the British army. Tallmadge knew when he saw Arnold's alias, Anderson, signed on the bottom of the incriminating documents.

from Woodhull which would be dead dropped in a wooden box kept in that field. From there, Roe would ride them on horseback to the necessary locations and recipients.

Brewster was a military man turned whaler, who used his whaling boats to move the Culper letters out of New York City. Brewster knew the geography and waters around the area, which allowed him to hide his boats in different coves around the city to avoid detection by the British and safely transport spy letters.

Strong, motivated by the incarceration of her military husband by the British, was a housewife and mother. Loyalist officers lived in the main house next to her cottage in Setauket, and she used her laundry line to foil the plots of the British who had imprisoned her husband. Strong would hang a black petticoat on her clothing line whenever Brewster pulled into a cove. As black petticoats were rare back then in that region, this would be a signal to Woodhull that Brewster was in one of the coves. Next to her petticoat she would hang anywhere from one to six different white handkerchiefs. The number of handkerchiefs would signal which cove Woodhull needed to go to meet and speak with Brewster.

Robert Townsend was the main source of intelligence in New York City. He ran a store and was a partner in a coffeehouse in New York. The British did not suspect Townsend to be a spy because he was also a Quaker—known pacifists who refused to take sides in the war. The British, however, did not know that Townsend felt bitter toward the British for the way they treated his family when he was a child. His profession as a store owner meant that many people would come into his store and share information. When it was relevant to the war, it was passed on through the ring to Washington.

Rivington was an unlikely spy for the patriots. He ran a loyalist, Tory newspaper and was Townsend's partner in the coffeehouse business. In the newspaper, Rivington spoke adamantly against the American cause and revolution, but behind closed doors he gave information to the patriots. Some historians think that Rivington may have switched from loyalist to patriot to protect his family when the tides of the war changed in favor of the Americans. Either way, he fed the Americans information and remained in the country after the war when many loyalists moved to Canada.

The Ring Foils a Plot

One of the biggest coups of the Culper Ring during the revolution came within August and September of

The Culper Cipher

The numbers used to designate different members of the Culper Spy Ring were part of a cipher that

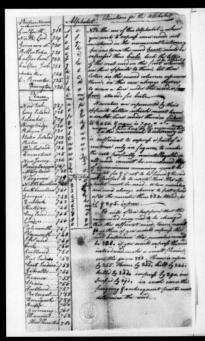

Tallmadge's cipher required a code dictionary to read the message.

Tallmadge created to protect the identities of his allies and confuse the British should they come upon a letter. Numbers stood in for different places and people so that any reader who did not know the code could not read the letter. New York City was denoted as 721 while Setauket was 729. There were 763 numbers used in the code. Members of the ring had what came to be called the code dictionary, which was a document that listed what the numbers equaled. The users would reference the code dictionary to decode letters. The code was based on *Entick's Spelling Dictionary*. Tallmadge, Washington, and Woodhull all used Tallmadge's code in their letters.

1778. The ring discovered that General Clinton was planning to send men to Newport, Rhode Island, to attack the French soldiers that had just arrived there. Washington was able to warn the French, and send false evidence back to the British that the Continental Army was planning an attack on New York. This redirected Clinton's attention away from Rhode Island.

The plan worked, tricking Clinton who called the troops on the way to Rhode Island back to New York to help defend the city. This protected the French who had only recently arrived in Rhode Island and were not ready to face an attack. Had they been attacked, the Americans might have lost much needed French support because the French would have pulled out of the war.

A Traitor in the Mix

The most infamous spy of the American Revolution is undoubtedly the traitorous Benedict Arnold. Prior to his betrayal, Arnold was an accomplished military man who won battles both on land and at sea for the Americans. He was prone to mood swings and began as a passionate patriot demanding American action after the Boston Massacre, but he was quick to temper and had too much pride.

Dissatisfied with the Dream

During the war, Arnold committed many acts of bravery. He was partially responsible for victory over the British at Fort Ticonderoga, which gave

Benedict Arnold conspired to surrender West Point to the British.

the Continental Army a strategic advantage; however, he was relieved of command over a political disagreement. Arnold was infuriated and refused to leave command until he was forced out. Then later, he was passed over for a promotion, and his pride was pricked.

He would later lead a foray into Canada along with General Richard Montgomery to storm Montreal and Quebec. Montgomery's troops captured Montreal, and came to aid with Arnold's efforts on Quebec. The Continental Army was not prepared and was horribly defeated. Montgomery died in battle. Arnold was heavily wounded, but it did not stop him from fighting all the way to the border. He was rewarded a promotion for his efforts and led the defense of Lake Champlain when the British retaliated. Unfortunately, Congress failed to recognize his efforts there and promoted other, less deserving officers ahead of Arnold.

Washington eventually forced Congress to give Arnold the promotion he deserved, but it was too late. Arnold was now ranked lower than those he was passed over for because Congress would not instate the promotion retroactively. He was insulted and resigned.

Washington talked Arnold into rejoining the military again. At that time he was sent to command troops under General Gates, but the two could not get along. Arnold continued to fight for the Americans, but he was again wounded in battle, this time with a musket bullet to the thigh, and could no longer fight. Washington granted him a desk job in May 1778 as the military commander in Philadelphia. Unfortunately for Arnold, his volatile temper was not well suited to rebuilding the recently retaken Philadelphia. To further exaggerate the problem, Arnold was out money. He was bitter toward Congress for the slights they had dealt him, and equally so for his current financial troubles. He made some very unwise financial decisions and ended up court-martialed by Washington himself for them. His life was near to ruin when Arnold fell in love with his future wife, socialite Peggy Shippen.

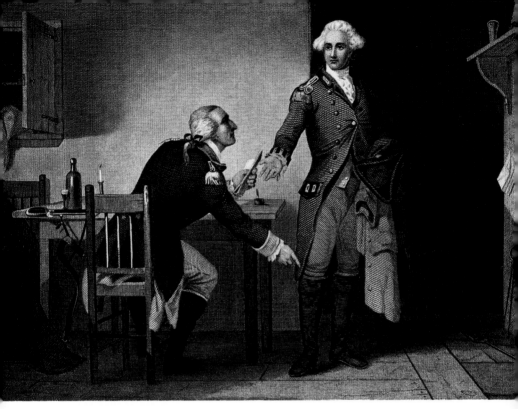

C. F. Blauvelt's *Treason of Arnold* shows Arnold betraying the Americans to Major André.

Turncoat

Shippen was good friends with many British officers and specifically British Major John André. When Washington dropped the charges against Arnold, Arnold felt cheated of his chance to defend himself and turned to the British, specifically André who was heading British intelligence in America.

André coordinated with Arnold, and Arnold agreed to surrender the strategically significant West Point to the British. Arnold gave André several top secret documents that explained how to win and take

African American Espionage

Both free African Americans and enslaved people took part in spying during the American Revolution. Unfortunately, due to racism and low literacy rates among slaves, not many of their stories were properly recorded. There are, however, a few whose tales have

A painting of Armistead and Lafayette

survived, like that of enslaved James Armistead, arguably one of the best spies under General Marquis de Lafayette.

Armistead posed as a runaway slave hired by the British to spy on Americans as a way to infiltrate the British army. He earned the trust of British General Charles Cornwallis, and pretended to ally with Benedict Arnold. During his service, Armistead provided information on British efforts to invade Yorktown toward the end of the war. Washington used this information to form a military blockade of American and French soldiers, which decimated British forces. The victory at Yorktown can be credited to Armistead, and it was that defeat which led the British to surrender on October 19, 1781.

After the war, Armistead was returned to slavery, but Lafayette helped him petition for his freedom, which he won in 1787. James Armistead changed his name to James Armistead Lafayette out of respect for the general he had served under.

the fort at West Point. There was also a plan devised to capture Washington at West Point.

It was during André's return trip from that meeting with Arnold that he was accidentally captured. He revealed himself as a British officer to a colonial solider dressed in a stolen British uniform. Arnold barely managed to escape when the documents carried by André were revealed to have been written by Arnold, but André was not so lucky.

Washington offered to trade André, who showed himself to be a true professional and honorable solider, for Arnold, the traitor. The British refused, fearing that turning over Arnold would discourage other American officers from defecting and turning to the British. André was executed as a spy. Arnold later took up arms against the patriots, but was never accepted by the British who saw him as a double traitor, first to England for his early service in the American military and then to the Americans for his later actions.

ESPIONGE: THEN AND NOW

Washington's role as a spy master and the men and women who spied for him are the reasons the Continental Army won the war. The legacy of these brave people was the founding of a nation. The Continental Army did not have the experience or power to defeat the British Army and its German allies. The colonial troops were less practiced at warfare and had fewer resources; they should not have won, but the patriots came prepared to fight for freedom by any means necessary. With proper and accurate military intelligence, along with the skillful leadership of Washington, they were able

OPPOSITE:
The Continental Army's triumph at Yorktown secured American victory over England.

to take on the British. As Major George Beckwith said at the close of the war, "Washington did not really outfight the British, he simply outspied [sic] us!"

The Legacy of the Revolution

Spying methods of the revolution were similar to those used previously in conflicts like the French and Indian War, but espionage became far more popular after this war. Spying was no longer a gentleman's game and was seen as sort of a disreputable career. As spying became dependent on subterfuge and secrets, it did not fit with the concepts of honor, truthfulness, and trustworthiness. Nevertheless, it was the established organizations like the Culper Ring that truly won the war, because those endeavors provided the most intelligence and information. It may have been a disrespected position to hold, but it was one of the most valued by Washington. The sheer necessity of spies during that conflict showed their value in war, and over time, the position has become one that deserves respect rather than rancor. Today, the men and women who risk their lives in service are exalted as war heroes, and the bravery of their actions is deeply respected.

In the past, especially prior to the American Revolution, espionage was primarily based around short forays into enemy territory. In this war, spying became a long game, one where spies spent months and even years imbedded in their positions or in disguise to ferret out information. The dusk to dawn spy missions were not as productive or effective. That does not mean that such missions ended, merely that spying was changing, and missions were much more complex. In many ways the revolution laid the groundwork for modern espionage.

Postwar Policies

The British continued sending spies even after the Treaty of Paris was signed, ending the war in 1783. Interest in America was still very prevalent and the hope of reestablishing control over the former colonies was not fully crushed until the War of 1812 was fought, and ended without the colonies returning to British control. Other nations still had a great deal of interest in the resources available in the Americas and the American colonies specifically. Nations like Great Britain kept spies to watch for weaknesses for years after the revolution.

Growing Within

The Americans, however, took a very different approach. George Washington operated the country with a closed-door policy and significantly less interest in foreign affairs. Focus was definitely turned inward toward building the nation and ensuring that independence was successful. Spies were not sent to other countries. That said, some of the committees and specialty departments created during the war with espionage in mind grew and were maintained even after the end of the war. For example, the Committee of Secret Correspondence would become the Committee for Foreign Affairs, which still operates today. While the Committee of Secret Correspondence was focused on espionage, the modern Committee for Foreign Affairs focuses on international relations and laws that relate to international relations. That committee investigates issues with foreign governments, watches out for America's foreign interests, and works to protect the country against international spies.

Washington also saw the value of information interests to help with securing the new nation's success. He took precautions to protect the new nation should it needs spies in the future. Washington requested that Congress establish a "secret service fund" during his first formal address to Congress. These funds were to be used for covert, secret missions. Congress granted the request and the fund was 10 percent of the federal budget. Funds procured by Washington would later

Jefferson and the Pirate States

Thomas Jefferson would be the first president to foray in any serious way outside of American borders while in office. In the face of rising tension with the

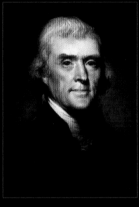

Thomas Jefferson was a Founding Father and the third president of the United States.

Barbary States, Jefferson was considering a coup. As one of the peace commissioners to the region, Jefferson was familiar with the area (a region in North Africa now known as Morocco, Libya, Tunisia, and Algeria), and the tensions surrounding the states. Without annuities in place with the Barbary States, an unprotected nation faced possible maritime trouble from marauders, as corsairs, or pirates, regularly attacked merchant ships. Since America had no such agreement, American shipping and trade interests were threatened.

Jefferson used the funds from the "secret service fund" to investigate possible options on how to solve the problem Barbary marauders posed to American shipping. Ultimately, Americans managed to work out a treaty, but the possibility of war was very real and could have had a dramatic effect on American diplomacy.

be used by presidents in the future. Thomas Jefferson would use the funds in his attempt to overthrow the Barbary Pirate states in Africa during his presidency. James Madison used it to employ agents while trying to persuade the Spanish to give up the Florida around 1810.

An Expensive Game

One could also trace the origins of the US National Security Agency (NSA) to the American Revolution through early code breakers Reverend Samuel West and Colonel Elisha Porter who broke the code on Benjamin Church's letter. Intelligence gathering began early in the war at the urgings of Washington, but the impact would be felt well into the future.

The seeds of early American intelligence and espionage have grown into a multibillion dollar industry in the modern world. The United States' 2018 budget requested $57.7 billion for the National Intelligence Program (NIS) and $20.7 billion for the Military Intelligence Program (MIP). That is $78.4 billion dedicated simply to gathering intelligence designed to protect the nation and country's assets. Organizations like the Federal Bureau of Investigation (FBI), the Central Intelligence Agency (CIA), and the Natural Security Agency (NSA) can find very early roots in the efforts of spies and code breakers during the American Revolution.

Though the formal establishment of these agencies would not come until much later in US history, there is no denying that American reliance on intelligence stems from efforts during the revolution. That early success as a result of spy efforts allowed for continued funding and the utilization of surveillance techniques in international and domestic interactions throughout American history. Funding and interest in intelligence would ultimately enable the founding of these organizations and investments in spy technologies. Today, the NSA performs international intelligence and counterintelligence, and works within the country to protect and maintain high-clearance classified information by breaking codes. It also works on designing and hacking some of the most complex computer encryptions used in the world.

Though it could not have been anticipated in 1776 with the start of the revolution that American's would become so dependent on espionage and intelligence gathering by the twenty first century, the American Revolution would not have been won without intelligence provided by spies and code breakers. The value of information was not lost on Washington or any future president of the United States. The astronomical amount of money contributed in 2018 to intelligence gathering shows the importance and dependence that the American government still has on information, spying, and codebreaking.

Treason During and After the War

The very act of the Founding Fathers sending the Declaration of Independence was an act of treason against Great Britain. They were betraying the mother country to found their own country. The Founding Fathers were not only facing death in war, but also by hanging or possibly death by being drawn and quartered for their treasonous act. Drawing and quartering was a brutal way to die where a person was tied to four different horses who all ran in different directions, tearing the person apart. It was a terrifying, gruesome, and horrific way to die. Spies were treated as traitors. Betraying the mother country could lead to a death sentence, more often by hanging.

Treason in the United States of America

Once independence was declared, a new nation was founded and new laws were passed by the states for dealing with their own traitors like Benedict Arnold and the spies who sold information to the British. At first, Pennsylvania simply imprisoned traitors, but the severity of the act was not reflected in the punishment. The consequences for treason quickly changed and escalated in 1777.

With the change, traitors were sentenced to death, and all of their assets became state property. A traitor was anyone who bought a commission in the British army, anyone who encouraged others to fight the Americans, and any person who aided or provided supplies to the enemy. Even Quakers who were staunchly pacifists by religious doctrine were looked on suspiciously for staying out of the war. It was a harsh punishment for any Tory sympathizer who may not have actively acted against the United States and such people who unintentionally aided the British. It did, however, seem to make sense when applied to spies and people who truly betrayed the new nation to Great Britain.

Ultimately, treason laws needed some revision though. A traitor was anyone who sided or remained loyal to the king in any capacity during and at the close of the war. All loyalists were considered treasonous and could technically be sentenced to death because of it. When the Constitution was written in 1787, the concept of treason was revised. A conviction needed at least two witnesses who could attest that a traitor had gone to war against the United States or explicitly aided the enemy before they could be condemned.

Spying After the Revolution

Spying took place again during the Civil War, and efforts picked up further during the Spanish American War at the turn of the nineteenth century. The methods used in the American Revolution would continue to evolve and be used well into the future.

Coding Information

Invisible ink continued to be improved and played an important role during World War I. Spies would send messages to one another using the secret ink that German chemists had created when other lemon juice inks had failed. Invisible inks were valuable as means to keep enemies from detecting sensitive information, and other nations took interest in invisible ink projects as well. The French and British, for example, worked

An Enigma coding machine from World War II

toward better and more efficient chemical inks to use and hide information with. Some of the methods and reagents used to make the inks visible still are not declassified to the general public even though World War I has been over for almost a century.

Codes and ciphers also continued to be used and improved drastically. The Soviet VIC Cipher used by the Soviet spy Reino Hayhanen during the Cold War was considered near to impossible to crack. It is still one of the most advanced ciphers discovered. The Americans were not able to break the cipher until Hayhanen defected in 1957 and came to the United States. As recently as 2016, it was determined that this incredibly complex cipher can only be cracked if the person knows the enciphering algorithm, which is very complex in itself. It put Tallmadge's much simpler cipher to shame.

The Dead Drop

One of the simplest methods used during the American Revolution has also been used as recently as the turn of the new millennium. Considered to be one of the most damaging spies in US history, Robert Phillip Hanssen used the dead drop to supply highly classified information to enemy states within the United States of America until his arrest in 2001.

Hanssen was working for Russia and the former Soviet Union by spying on the United States. His career as a counterintelligence agent for the FBI gave him access to incredible amounts of politically and internationally sensitive, classified, and valuable information. Ironically, he managed to steal and trade such carefully guarded secrets with one of the most basic methods of espionage.

Hanssen would seal the classified information and dead drop it under a footbridge in Virginia's Foxstone Park for pick up by the SVR and eventually the KGB. Hanssen provided information to Russia and the former Soviet Union for twenty-two years and made more than $600,000 in cash and diamonds for his betrayal. Though seemingly an antiquated method of espionage used during the American Revolution, the dead drop made him rich, and is still a utilized technique today.

Modern Encryption Used Everyday

Modern online shops, banks, and credit score sites also draw on methods to keep secrets that were used in the American Revolution. The techniques for encoding information, such as that used in letters during the revolution, are very simple forms of the modern encryptions financial institutions have in place to protect customers' data. Complex and challenging cipher codes stand between hackers and individuals' personal financial information. While the

Modern banking software uses complex codes like this to conceal and protect personal information.

technology in this sector has improved astronomically since the early days of the revolution, the concept is the same: making the information harder to read protects it from enemy eyes. Modern hackers have to work through obstacles like firewalls, passwords, and data protection software in the same way code breakers had to work with masks, ciphers, and spy networks to uncover wanted information.

A Nation Founded on Spies

In many ways, America is founded on the intrigue of spies and code breakers. Without the efforts of his spy network, Washington's army did not stand a chance against the British superpower. That tradition lives on today with organizations like the CIA and FBI that use intelligence to protect the interests of the United States from internal and international threats. Though new technologies far exceed the limitations and even the imaginations of the Founding Fathers and early spies, examples of the early spy methods are still seen and used in modern espionage. The revolution ended in 1783, but the national dependence on military and international intelligence has only grown as American faces new and modern threats like terrorism and nuclear weapons.

Washington worked hard to be one step ahead of his enemy as often as possible, and those efforts won him the revolution. Today, the need for information and intelligence has only increased. Though the threats and enemies are different from those that our Founding Fathers faced, the need to be one step ahead of the threat continues.

Chronology

1753 George Washington inherits his late brother's officer's commission in the British military and carries a letter for Governor Robert Dinwiddie to the French.

1754 The British lose to the French captain Louis Coulson at Fort Necessity.

1755 Washington acts as aid-de-camp to Major General Edward Braddock. The two lose in an ambush by the French and Native Americans because they had insufficient intelligence about the area and French military.

1765 England passes the Stamp Act in order to help cover some of the costs accrued during the French and Indian War. Protests break out in the colonies. The act is repealed.

1766 The Declaratory Act is passed to reestablish British control over the American colonies.

1767 Parliament passes the Townsend Acts placing a duty on paint, lead, glass, paper, and tea in the colonies. They are met with a lot of people protesting taxation without representation in Parliament.

1770 All duties save the tea duty from the Townsend Acts are repealed.

1773 The Tea Act grants exclusive tea trade with the colonies to the East India Company. Massachusetts colonists protest the Tea Act by tossing 342 chests of East India Company tea into the Boston Harbor during the Boston Tea Party.

1774 The Coercive Acts are passed to punish the Boston colony for the actions of the Boston Tea Party.

1775 Silas Dean and Dr. Edward Bancroft are working in France. Dean is negotiating with the French. Bancroft is suppling intelligence to the British about those negotiations. Washington enlists William Duer to form a spy network in and around British New York.

1776 Nathan Hale is executed as a spy.

1777 The Clark Spy Ring operates in Philadelphia.

1778 Franklin secures French support and alliance in the American Revolution. The Culper Spy Ring begins operating in Long Island and New York under Benjamin Tallmadge. The Culper Spy Ring provides information that spoils General Clinton's plan to attack the French in Rhode Island.

1780 Benedict Arnold betrays the Americans at West Point. British Major John André is hanged for his conspiring with Arnold over West Point.

1781 James Armistead alerts Washington of British plans for Yorktown, leading to the battle that essentially ends the war.

1783 The Treaty of Paris is signed, ending the American Revolution.

Glossary

black chamber A room designated for espionage where letters from enemies were opened, read, and copied for spying purposes.

cipher The act of changing a text and coding it to make it more challenging to read; can also be the document that is the end product of such encoding.

closed-door policy When a country does not allow other people into the country, especially concerning foreign affairs, trade, and military action.

code A system where numbers, symbols, or letters stand in for words and other ideas to confuse an enemy and keep the secrets out of the hands of the enemy.

code dictionary The document used by members of the Culper Spy Ring to decode the letters sent between members.

commission A purchased document that declared a man as an officer in the British military.

Culper Spy Ring A spy ring working under George Washington between 1778 and 1783 out of Setauket, New York, and providing information about the British occupations of the Long Island and New York City areas.

dead drop An espionage act where one spy leaves documents or information in a predetermined location for another agent to pick up at a later time.

East India Trading Company A British charter company that enabled trade with the East Indies.

encryption To encipher or code a document so that others will not be able to read it.

espionage The act or use of spying, especially by military and government agencies.

hacker A person who understands computers very well and can use that knowledge to break through firewalls and decode computer encryptions.

intelligence Information gathered about the enemy and used to make strategic military movements.

masks Otherwise known as grilles. A paper with a custom cutout that was placed over a spy letter to help the recipient view the concealed message.

petticoat A underskirt or slip that women wore under their skirts.

propaganda Information spread to work against and harm the reputation and support for a political enemy.

quill A bird feather, often from a goose, that is used as a pen.

reconnaissance Gathering military intelligence while fighting and in the field.

Sons of Liberty Many different secret organizations that became public. They spoke out against the Stamp Act and pushed for American independence during the revolution.

sympathetic stain A chemically reactive invisible ink designed by James Jay and used by the Culper Spy Ring and George Washington during the American Revolution.

Tory An American colonist who supported England during the American Revolution, also known as a loyalist.

Further Information

Books

Allen, Thomas B. *George Washington, Spymaster: How Americans Outspied the British and Won the Revolutionary War.* Washington DC: National Geographic, 2004.

Buranelli, Vincent. *American Spies and Traitors.* New York: Enslow Publishers, 2004.

Edwards, Roberta. *Who Is George Washington?* New York: Grosset & Dunlap, 2009.

Raum, Elizabeth. *Spies of the American Revolution: an Interactive Espionage Adventure.* North Mankato, MN: Capstone Press, 2016.

Sheinkin, Steve. *The Notorious Benedict Arnold.* New York: Roaring Book Press, 2010.

Websites

Benjamin Franklin: World Spies

http://www.pbs.org/benfranklin/ l3_world_spies.html

Explore Benjamin Franklin's spying efforts during the American Revolution more fully with this brief biography.

CIA— Kids Zone

https://www.cia.gov/kids-page/6-12th-grade/
operation-history/revolutionary-war.html

*See the spy efforts of the Revolution described in first
person point of view from some of the most influential
participants of the American Revolution.*

"The Culper Spy Ring"

https://www.youtube.com/watch?v=tCId5Un7ZxA
"The Culper Spy Ring" by Shelly Steglich

*This short documentary provides a great overview of
the participants in the Culper Spy Ring and their actions
taken while a part of it.*

**"Nine Women Who Helped Win
the American Revolution"**

http://mentalfloss.com/article/67905/9-women-
who-helped-win-american-revolution

*Some of the female spies and women of the revolution
come alive in these brief biographies.*

Selected Bibliography

Andrews, Evan. "5 Patriot Spies of the American Revolution." *History.com*. October 20, 2015. http://www.history.com/news/history-lists/5-patriot-spies-of-the-american-revolution.

Biography.com Editors. "James Armistead Biorgraphy.com." *Biograpy.com*. Last modified September 12, 2016. https://www.biography.com/people/james-armistead-537566.

The Culper Ring: the History and Legacy of the Revolutionary War's Most Famous Spy Ring. Lexington, KY: Charles River Publishers, 2015.

Daigler, Kenneth A. *Spies, Patriots, and Traitors: American Intelligence in the Revolutionary War*. Washington DC: Georgetown University Press, 2014.

Fischer, David Hackett. *Paul Revere's Ride*. New York: Oxford University Press, 1994.

Hardy, Rob. "Reveal: a History of Hidden Writing." *The Dispatch*. September 12, 2014. https://cdispatch.com/robhardy/article.asp?aid=36284

Huff, Elizabeth, and Priscilla and Richard Roberts. "The First Barbary War." The Jefferson Monticello. https://www.monticello.org/site/research-and-collections/first-barbary-war.

Kilmeade, Brian, and Don Yaeger. *Washington's Secret Six: The Spy Ring that Saved the American Revolution*. New York: Sentinel, 2014.

Mount Vernon Ladies' Association. "George Washington's Mount Vernon." Mountvernon.org. http://www.mountvernon.org.

Mount Vernon Ladies' Association. "Spy Techniques of the Revolutionary War." Mountvernon.org. http://www.mountvernon.org/george-washington/ the-revolutionary-war/spying-and-espionage/spy-techniques-of-the-revolutionary-war.

Nagy, John A. *Washington's Secret Spy War: The Making of America's First Spymaster*. New York: St. Martin's Press, 2016.

Nyitray, Kristen. "George Washington and the Culper Spy Ring: Home." *Stony Brook University Libraries*. http://guides.library.stonybrook.edu/culper-spy-ring.

Roberts, Sam. "War of Secrets; Spy History 101: America's Intelligence Quotient." *New York Times*. September 8, 2002. http://www.nytimes.com/2002/09/08/weekinreview/war-of-secrets-spy-history-101-america-s-intelligence-quotient.html?mcubz=1.

Rose, Alexander. *Washington's Spies: the Story of America's First Spy Ring.* New York: Bantam Dell, 2006.

Rose, P.K. "The Founding Fathers of American Intelligence." Central Intelligence Agency. https://www.cia.gov/library/center-for-the-study-of-intelligence/csi-publications/books-and-monographs/the-founding-fathers-of-american-intelligence/art-1.html.

"Secret Committee of Correspondence/Committee for Foreign Affairs, 1775-1777." Department of State Office of the Historian. https://history.state.gov/milestones/1776-1783/secret-committee.

Sulick, Michael J. *Spying in America: Espionage from the Revolutionary War to the Dawn of the Cold War.* Washington DC: Georgetown University Press, 2012.

Taylor & Francis. "Cold War Russian Cipher May Finally Be Solved." *Science Daily.* February 2, 2016. https://www.sciencedaily.com/releases/2016/02/160202122506.htm.

Index

About the Author

Cassandra Schumacher is a writer from Western New York with a bachelor's degree in anthropology and creative writing from the State University of New York at Oswego. She has a particular fondness for cooking on Sunday afternoons, petting every dog she sees, and hanging out with her three leopard geckos.